John M. jr Way, John Way

Guide to Moosehead lake and Northern Maine

John M. jr Way, John Way

Guide to Moosehead lake and Northern Maine

ISBN/EAN: 9783741103148

Manufactured in Europe, USA, Canada, Australia, Japa

Cover: Foto ©ninafisch / pixelio.de

Manufactured and distributed by brebook publishing software
(www.brebook.com)

John M. jr Way, John Way

Guide to Moosehead lake and Northern Maine

GUIDE

TO

Moosehead Lake,

AND

NORTHERN MAINE.

BOSTON.
BRADFORD & ANTHONY,
186 Washington Street,
1874.

CONTENTS.

MOOSEHEAD LAKE.

———

NORTHERN MAINE,

Or Tours beyond the Lake.

———

MOOSEHEAD LAKE.

ON the outskirts of the unbroken wilderness of Northern Maine lies an expansive sheet of crystal water, forty miles in length, three to fifteen miles in width, and containing a surface of one hundred and twenty square miles. It is the great reservoir that supplies the wild and picturesque Kennebec, and renders accessible its mightier neighbor, the famous Penobscot. Islands, varying in size from the lonely rock to those of miles in extent, with hills and valleys of their own, rest upon its bosom. Mountains, too, in isolated peaks and detached groups, either frown upon its borders or skirt the horizon, shrouded in a rich blue haze. Its shores, tortuous and winding, are one continuous forest, where all the larger varieties of game abound. But the excellent trout fishing is the great attraction, both in the lake itself and on its many tributaries, ever varied and picturesque.

ROUTES FROM BOSTON.

I.

BY RAIL VIA BANGOR TO GUILFORD.

Round Trip, $15.00; Single Ticket, $8.50, — Good by
either Route.

6.20 P. M., Eastern Railroad to Guilford, . . 307 miles.
11 A. M., Stage to Greenville, ... 25 "
4 P. M., Steamer to Mt. Kineo, ... 20 "

6 P. M., Arrival in twenty-four hours, . . . 352 "

This route accommodates the night travel and
saves a day's time. It may be varied by leaving
Boston at 8.15 A. M., and passing the night in
Bangor. Sleeping cars are provided on the
night train. Cars changed at Bangor. Breakfast taken in Bangor, and dinner at Monson.

II.

BY RAIL TO DEXTER.

Round Trip, $15.00; Single Ticket, $8.50, — Good by
either Route.

8.15 A. M., Eastern Railroad to Dexter, . . . 233 miles.
8 A. M., Stage to Greenville, (next day,) . . . 35 "
4 P. M., Steamer to Mt. Kineo, ... 20 "

6 P. M., Arrival in thirty-four hours, ... 288 "

This route is the most direct, but does not make connection with the night express. Cars are changed at Newport, and the night is passed in Dexter at a good hotel. Breakfast is obtained at Dexter and dinner at Monson.

III.

BY STEAMER TO BANGOR AND RAIL TO GUILFORD.

Round Trip, $13.00.
Tickets to Greenville, $6.00 ; Steamer to Mt. Kineo, $1.00 = $7.00.

MONDAYS, TUESDAYS, THURSDAYS, AND FRIDAYS.

First Day—5 P. M., Rowe's Wharf, Sanford's Line.
Second Day—12 M., Arrival in Bangor, . . . 235 miles.
Third Day—7 A.M., European R'way to Guilford, 61 "
   " —11 A. M., Stage to Greenville,. . . 25 "
   " —4 P. M., Steamer to Mt. Kineo, . . 20 "
   " —6 P. M., Arrival in forty-nine hours, 341 "

This route includes a delightful sail up the Penobscot river, and ample time to view the pleasing little city of Bangor, with its quiet homes and shaded streets. There is a train that leaves Bangor for Guilford at 5.10 P. M., but no time will be saved by it, unless a private conveyance is taken early the next morning, from the latter place.

THE RETURN TRIP. — The steamer leaves the Mt. Kineo House in season to connect by stage with the cars at Guilford or Dexter, and reach Boston early the next morning.

Breakfast may be obtained at Greenville, dinner at Guilford, and supper at Dexter or Newport by the first route, and in Bangor by the second and third.

The Sanford steamers leave Bangor for Boston on Mondays, Wednesdays, Thursdays, and Saturdays, at 11 A. M.

THE STAGE RIDE.—All the routes converge at or near Guilford, and the stages stop for dinner at Monson, this season, but sometimes at Guilford or Abbot. The road follows first the pleasant valley of the Piscataquis, then traverses the country to Monson, well known for its slate quarries. Off to the left rises Russell Mountain, over the notch in which the old stage road from Skowhegan climbs, now but little used except to carry the mail for the farming towns on the way. Fresh horses at Monson prepare us for the famous Doughty Hill, so much dreaded during the snows of winter and the fall mud, but utterly impassable during the thaws of April. Soon after leaving Monson the lofty mountains about

the Lake crowd upon the view, and a short ride
of fourteen miles brings us to Greenville, a
farming town of several hundred inhabitants,
with two good hotels. Here a steamer is in
readiness to cross

THE LAKE.

EAVING Greenville we soon thread our way among the many islands, and gaze once more with admiration upon old Squaw Mountain, as we meet it face to face. Passing Ledge Island, the last of the smaller ones, we look off into Sandy Bay, while up to the right and rear of us is the McFarland Place, with its fine view, surpassed in magnitude by that from Mt. Kineo, but not in beauty by any in Northern Maine. On the left comes Moose Island, a sort of hermit's retreat At present, John Cusac keeps bachelor's hall in a comfortable log cabin, on its western shore, and in a spacious barn cares tenderly for a fine herd of live stock. Beyond the clearing, on Burnt Jacket, we espy the narrows, near Garland's place, that lead into Lily Bay. One mile east of the channel, and eight from Greenville, is Birch Island, a delightful spot, and one of the few smaller islands that has retained its primitive growth beyond the reach of the rise of water occasioned by the building of a dam eight feet high, at the outlet.

The Deer Island House, a good place for summer boarders, is now in full view before us.

The accommodating spirit which lands passengers at any desired point on the route, would
not disappoint them here.

Passing between Deer and Sugar Islands, we
find ourselves in the midst of the broadest part
of the lake, which fades away in the dim distance to the east. There lies Spencer Bay, and
beyond, rising, as it were, from a plain to the
height of 4050 feet, are the two Spencer Mountains. At the base of the more northerly is
Spencer Pond, noted for its fishing, while beyond, on their right, Mt. Katahdin, of which
we caught a glimpse farther down the lake, is
distinguished by the land slide on its face. Four
miles to the westward of the channel the Outlet
House raises its white wall against the horizon
at the Kennebec Dam, the outlet of the lake and
the never-failing resort of fishermen.

First, Hog Back, then Sand Bar Islands disappear. West of the latter is the Sand Bar
Farm, four miles from the outlet, where John
Masterman, an old trapper, entertains his guests
with his rare experience. Comfortable quarters,
pleasant surroundings, and modest charges are
its attractious. Next comes the East Outlet, the
smaller and a tributary of the West Outlet. By
a strange freak of nature, the lake possesses

two outlets, which unite at a distance of some miles.

Mt. Kineo House now confronts us, a few miles distant, and at its rear the sheer precipice of nearly eight hundred feet, that gives it its name. The steamer touches at the wharf, and we hurry in to a hot supper.

Several times a week the boat leaving Greenville in the morning, continues its way to the North East Carry at the head of the lake.

After leaving the Mt. Kineo House it rounds the point of the mountain, from which the ascent is made, and passes on the left the mouth of Moose River on the north side of the Blue Ridge. Then comes Farm Island, and beyond it Socatean Bay, into which empties the river of the same name, with its picturesque falls.

We are now in North Bay, a fine sheet of water stretching sixteen miles in a straight course, and several miles in width. Its eastern shore is skirted by low ranges of hills, while the Spencers and Katahdin loom up in the back ground, grander than before. The Shaw farm, which raises oats and hay in abundance, for lumbermen, and Duck Cove, the only break on that side, attract our attention. On the west,

beyond the clearing, now abandoned, called W
Farm, is Williams Stream, where there is a
never-failing supply of the smallest brook trout,
the sweetest in flavor of the trout species. At
times, when the larger fish retire from the heat
to deep water, these little fellows crowd for safety to the cool shades of this spring brook.

At the head of the bay, at the north-west angle
of the lake, is the North West Carry, across which
lies the course of those who ascend the West
Branch of the Penobscot to pass into Canada, or
to cross over to Baker Lake, on the South Branch
of the St. John. Uncle Marsh Lane, an old lumberman, tills a small farm here, and sometimes
hauls canoes over the rough carry road. Carry
Brook, near by, is well worth a visit on account
of its falls, twelve feet in height, and three miles
from the lake.

But the steamer's destination is the North East
Carry, at the other angle of the lake, and so we
pass on to the low sandy reach in front of the
Carry House, and anchor at some distance from
the shore. In August, multitudes flock to this
spot from all the country towns below Greenville
to camp out and pick blueberries. The country
having been burnt over some years since, blueberries have sprung up in abundance. It is a

source of profit to some, but to most the great recreation of the year.

The Carry is a great thoroughfare for lumbermen in winter, and for tourists in summer. It is two miles and forty rods in length. Mr. Morris with his team, awaits the arrival of the boat to haul canoes and luggage across to the West Branch. Nearly all the travel beyond the lake passes this way, to Chesuncook and Chamberlain Lakes, to the Allagash and St. John Rivers, to Katahdin and elsewhere. But to return to the foot of the Lake.

GREENVILLE,

SNUG little village lies nestled by the shore at the head of a narrow cove, its quiet harbor sheltered from the main body of the lake by numerous islands and headlands. To the northwest Squaw Mountain looms up, surrounded by a host of spurs and lesser heights, while homesteads, neat and tidy with all the signs of New England thrift, stretch away upon the hillside to the south and east. A modest church with belfry tower, a town hall with schoolroom beneath, two hotels, (the Eveleth and the Lake House,) two stores and a steam saw mill, comprise its business centre. It derives its support from the lumbering interest, which takes the farmers' surplus and drains the extra labor of the place.

There are many pleasant rambles in this neighborhood, including that to West Cove. Within a radius of twelve miles are no less than twenty ponds, by actual count. The walks and drives are of the first order, and we will commence with the view from

THE McFARLAND PLACE,

By many considered the finest on the Lake. It is two miles and a half northeast of the village, by a good carriage road, and Mr. Mitchell, of the Eveleth House, is always ready to take his guests up there. It is said that we obtain the best idea of height from a point where we can look both up and down. This is one advantage here, but the peculiar charm lies in the broken aspect of the lake : land and water, height and valley, being mingled in great confusion ; and in front lies a broad sheet of water, stretching away to Deer Island. Over a neck of land, to the northeast of this, we see Beaver Cove. Separated by another piece of woodland lies Lily Bay, while beyond, in the far distance, is Spencer Bay, with its noble mountains. Squaw Mountain, Moose Island, and Mt. Kineo, also appear, but need no mention here.

WILSON PONDS.

But the one special attraction for sportsmen is the fishing in the Wilson Ponds. The nearer and larger of these is three miles from the lake, two of which are by a good road. The last mile crosses Mr. Cummings's farm, and then descends

through the woods, steep and rough, to the lake.
It is customary to leave the horse with Mr. Cummings or send him back to the hotel, and proceed
on foot. On a knoll in the clearing, by the crest
of the hill, is the Swiss pavilion of our friend
and fellow sportsman, Mr. G. G. Grennell, of
New York. Attracted to the spot by the beauty.
of the scenery, the abundance of its game, and
the variety of its sports, he lingers through the
Indian summer of each season.

In a deep basin lies the pond, enclosed by high
mountains, where many a sequestered pool conceals its trout. Many boats are on the shore, and
the fishing is done in comparatively deep water,
with the angle worm for bait. Usually a guide
is taken from Greenville, but Mr. Ivory Littlefield, of the Lake House, takes pleasure in conducting his guests there without extra charge.

Connected by its outlet, half a mile in length,
and three miles distant from where we reach the
Lower, is the Upper Wilson. It is a trip that
necessitates camping out in order to do much
fishing. In this case, Bonner Mountain, on its
eastern shore, will well repay a visit.

EAGLE STREAM.

Two miles from the lake a small trout brook wanders through an open meadow, affording the best of chances to cast a fly. Those who prefer to ride can, by a longer route, approach within half a mile. There is no better eating than these smallest fish, and scarce any finer sport. Angle worms are also used as bait.

SQUAW MOUNTAIN.

As far as known, the height of this grand old pile has never been estimated. The lake is a thousand feet above the sea, and, judging from other heights in its vicinity, this can, by no possibility, be less than three thousand feet. With guides and canoes, the party proceeds to Squaw Brook, five miles distant. A mile up the brook, Fitzgerald Pond lies under the shadow of the mountain. It is usually necessary to carry canoes most of the way from the lake to the pond. On its farther shore, in an old building, used only in the haying season, is the place to camp. In the following day the party ascends, and if not too tired, returns to Greenville.

THE OUTLET.

TWELVE miles from Greenville is a resort by itself, and the surest fishing ground in these waters. Thousands of pounds are caught annually, but the supply is unlimited. The fish average two or more pounds, but many weigh four and five. During the hot weather they are quite small. Both bait and fly are used. The fishing is done generally from the dam, night and morning being the best time.

Close at hand Henry Wilson has erected a neat two story and a half house, and furnishes good food and shelter at moderate prices. Gentlemen resort here mostly, though ladies are often accommodated. Steamers run in here four miles to oblige passengers, with little or no extra charge. Without a guide and at less expense than at the hotels, one can pass a few days here very pleasantly. Several ponds are not far distant, in the interior.

MT. KINEO,

HE chief point of interest lies in the centre of the lake. At its base is situated the Mt. Kineo House, a first-class hotel, furnishing all of the comforts and most of the luxuries of its city rivals. Within two hours' sail from Greenville, by steamer, and within twenty-two hours from Boston, it is at the same time one of the most isolated and one of the most accessible of inland resorts.

One hundred and fifty guests have often been accommodated at this hotel. A spacious dining hall, its billiard hall, private parlors, and verandas, render it cheering and social in the gloomiest of weather. Boats are plenty, and many of the best guides make the hotel their headquarters. The steamer Day Dream takes out parties at reasonable rates, to sail around the mountain, or make other short excursions. It may also be hired for longer trips at ten dollars per day.

Back of the hotel shady paths wind through the grove to Pebbly Beach. There the east end of Mt. Kineo, from a height of seven hundred and eighty-nine feet, overhangs water of unknown depth, no bottom having been reached at several hundred feet. Eagles scream about the precipice, and the little Day Dream comes here to blow its whistle and try the echo. By the side of the deep water, at a short distance from the shore, is Table Rock, a favored spot for the fly-fishermen of the house.

Out in the lake, half a mile west from the hotel, and anchored in sixty feet of water, is the buoy, a small float, used to fasten boats to for fishing. The spot is kept well-baited, to attract the large fish that lie near the bottom. They are a species of trout, distinguished by a forked tail and the absence of red spots among the yellow ones on the belly. They average five pounds in weight, but are caught each year weighing sixteen, while they have been known to reach twenty-five and over. Besides these, there is the white fish, averaging one and a half pounds, and formerly thought never to exceed two, but within a few years several have been taken weighing three and four. Biting gently at such a depth, it requires an expert fisherman to hook them, but they are a delicate fish, and if only slightly pricked are soon seen floating on the surface. Though rather oily to the taste, they are by some considered superior to any trout.

A few of the principal excursions that may be made from the Mt. Kineo House are next given.

THE ASCENT OF MT. KINEO.

A boat is required to row to the western end of the mountain, one mile distant. Thence it is a rough but not difficult path, always on the brink of the precipice, and in full view of the house to the summit.

The ascent requires from thirty to sixty minutes, according to the party. Ladies accomplish it readily by taking time. In the slight depression between the two crests on top, a little spring of pure water trickles out of the rock.

Once on the summit, the most extended view greets the gaze. By the aid of our map one can decipher every body of water and most of the mountains. Suffice it to say that scarce a corner of the lake remains concealed, while the country for miles around presents itself to view.

There is another path leading up the face of the cliff, back of the hotel, but it is quite difficult, and intended for the venturesome only.

MISERY STREAM.

Enters Brassua Lake near its outlet, seven miles from Kineo. Numbers of large fish lie in the spring holes near the mouth. The journey to and from forms no small part of the attrac.

tion, and presents a pleasing variety. Two miles
of it lie across Moosehead, four up Moose River,
and one across Brassua Lake. The last half of
the distance on Moose River is quick water,
rocky and picturesque. Sportsmen usually walk
along the shore while the guide poles the canoe
up the rapids.

SOCATEAN RIVER,

Eight miles from Kineo, is a narrow stream,
dark and deep, and winding between banks of a
rich green foliage. It was once a famous moose
ground, and even now is occasionally visited,
while bears roam undisturbed through its soli-
tudes. Four miles from the lake a picturesque
cascade breaks over a sharp ledge, while numbers of small trout sport themselves in the pool
beneath.

East of its mouth, in the deep shade of a
spruce grove, a family party from Boston found
pleasant camping ground, a few years since,
erecting a cabin of spruce bark, and shelters of
the same for dining hall and cook house. Tents
were pitched, a hammock suspended, and a fire-
place elaborately constructed of smooth rocks.
The forest was cleared of its underbrush, and

steps led down the bank to the landing on the beach. Seats under the trees looked out upon the water, where a sail boat rode at anchor; while in canoes well filled, the ladies, the children, and all, cruised upon the river or coasted along the shore.

SPENCER POND,

A famous fishing ground, the home of the black duck, and the scene of a wild marshy vegetation, almost tropical in luxuriance. It is the remotest point on the lake, and its outlet, one mile and a half in length, empties into Spencer Bay, fifteen miles from Kineo and twenty from Greenville. It is a long paddle by canoe, particularly in windy weather, and the use of a sail boat is advisable.

In low water the guide wades up the stream with the canoe, and the sportsman walks up the old road, shooting partridges.

The pond itself is nearly circular, and a mile and a half in diameter. The bottom is a bed of soft mud, where numerous aquatic plants take root, covering the surface and blossoming in profusion. Sweetest among them all is the pond lily, a delicate flower with tremendous

roots. Some strips of cranberry meadow along
the shore are a floating bog, that rises and falls
with the water. Hid among the bulrushes the
muskrat begins early in the fall to build its
house of mud and sticks, in shape like a bee-
hive, oftentimes as large. Blue herons, quaint
and solitary, wing their way from hassock to
hassock; eagles perch upon the tree-tops, and
owls are often heard hooting in the distance.
Flock after flock of wild ducks rises and floats
away when disturbed. The time has been when
moose thronged its shores, and even now they
stray in each season.

Spencer Mountain, about a mile distant, is
difficult of access, it being necessary to make a
circuit in order to avoid the precipices that face
the pond. The ascent is rarely made. A few
sportsmen have been up; and Old Ellis, the
noted trapper, is said to have been the first to
try it.

In the mouths of two brooks at the north and
east ends of the pond, are deep spring holes,
with gravelly bottoms. Here the trout are found
from the smallest to those weighing three pounds
or more.

Little Spencer, a quiet pool, lies hid among
the hills, a mile away, on the north brook.

ROACH RIVER and LUCKY POND, also in Spencer Bay, are worthy of notice. At certain seasons numbers of trout lie in a pool half a mile from the mouth of the former, while the shallow and marshy character of the latter invites swarms of black ducks, and deer have lately made it a resort.

MOOSE RIVER,

The real Kennebec, is the only tributary of Moosehead Lake that is navigable for any considerable distance, while the main Kennebec is too rough. It presents a charming variety, and is ascended without the labor of the longer carriers found on the other routes, there being only one of half a mile below Long Lake, and that not always used. Under the head of Misery Stream the first part of the trip has already been described. Thirty miles from Kineo is the bridge where the Canada road crosses the stream. Half of this distance lies across lakes each differing from the last in size and appearance. Deer are plenty about Brassua Lake, and muskrats, ducks, loons, herons, gulls, and partridges are constantly met with. On Long Pond are two farms, and at the bridge a small settlement, with a custom house. Wood and Altean Ponds, lying beyond, are worthy of a visit.

GENERAL INFORMATION.

STEAMERS.

Two large steamboats, the Gov. Coburn and the Fairy of the Lake, of from sixty to ninety tons burthen, are in constant use upon the lake. Beside these there is the Lumberman, also quite large, and used only in the spring and fall. Their great size is due to the heavy work that they are called upon to perform. From the middle of May till the last of June they tow large rafts of logs to be sluiced through the dam and floated down the Kennebec. In October and November load after load of men, horses, and freight crosses the lake to the forests beyond. During the summer season some scattering freight and the usual travel keep them busy until the rush in blueberry time.

Two others, the Twilight and Day Dream, both quite small, complete the list. The one is a passenger boat, and runs regularly to Mt. Kineo and the head of the lake. The other is a pleasure yacht, stationed at the Mt. Kineo House, and referred to under that head.

SAIL BOATS.

The most satisfactory way to enjoy the lake is with sail boat and canoe. A party of from two to six, with two guides, two canoes, and a large sail boat, may cruise leisurely from point to point, with supplies in abundance, stop at the various logging camps, or pitch tent and enjoy themselves hugely. With more than two the shooting is done at a disadvantage, while six is a crowd ; and though they may oftentimes fish all at once, yet they must derive their sport mostly from each other's society, and perhaps that is the best of all, particularly when gathered in the ample space of a large logging camp, among lively companions.

First upon the list we would mention the yacht Challenge, of about eight tons burthen and twenty-six feet keel, owned by Capt. Samuel Cole. It may be obtained, with a complete camp outfit, two reliable guides, and two canoes, for eight dollars per day ; or with one guide for six dollars ; five dollars for long trips. All engagements should be made some weeks in advance.

Next in order, but a third smaller, is the neat centre-board boat of Capt. Frank Vaughn, and the price for himself and one canoe is five dollars per day.

The sloop Dauntless is owned by Capt. SAMUEL COLE. There are several other smaller craft about the lake, including the Comet, owned by DANIEL S. HARRINGTON, and let without guide for one dollar per day.

A few *row boats*, chiefly at Kineo for the use of the guests, are employed for short trips and deep-water fishing. But

CANOES

Are the chief mode of conveyance. Made by Indians, of birch bark, and lined with cedar, they are eighteen feet long, three wide, round up alike at each end, and weigh from seventy-five to one hundred pounds when perfectly dry. They are propelled by one paddle at the stern, and often another at the bow. They cost about twenty dollars, last from three to ten years, according to quality and usage, and may be hired of D. T. SANDERS & Co., Greenville, for twenty-five cents per day. Also, Capt. Samuel Cole generally has some to spare. Most of the guides are provided.

In the hands of inexperienced persons there is not only great danger of upsetting, but even the canoe itself is liable to much damage, for the bark is easily broken and soon leaks. Properly handled, it should never touch any stick or stone, nor even grate on the sand, but be "waded" ashore, and carefully lifted out, high and dry. In the summer season they are the only means of transit through the wilderness beyond the lake, and without them there would be less fur to supply the market and less known about the waters of the State.

There is a flat-bottomed boat called *bateau*, and used by the river-drivers only, but from four to six men are necessary to carry one.

GUIDES.

There are upwards of a score of able-bodied men about the lake, mostly trappers, some French Canadians, and a few Indians, inured to hardship and reared in the woods, who conduct the traveller from point to point. The greater part reside at Greenville, and receive their letters there, but many make the Mt. Kineo House their headquarters for the season. They furnish, generally, a canoe and cooking tools, and their wages are three dollars per day, although some get three and a half for trips on the river.

For convenience of reference we give below the names of a few of the older guides. Others equally deserving might be added :

SAMUEL COLE,	FRANK VAUGHN,
DAN. S. HARRINGTON,	JOHN SWAN,
CHARLES MESERVEY,	SIMON CAPINO,
ED. G. MASTERMAN,	JOHN L. MASTERMAN,
LOUIS KETCHUM,	SAMUEL DUTTON,
JASON A. HAMILTON,	JAMES BOWLEY,
FRANK WILLER,	NAHUM SMITH,
JOHN HALL,	JOHN R. COOMBS,
JOE CROSS,	PETER RONCOE.

OUTFIT.

The usual blue flannel or brown water-proof shirt, woolen drawers, overalls or pants of strong material, stout water-tight boots, socks, broad-brimmed felt hat, and frock or coat are a sportsman's dress. A small compass, a water-proof match-box, and a stout jack-knife are essential. A map is convenient.

For fire-arms, breech-loaders are preferable. Allen's double-barrelled shot gun, size No. 10, happens to be the favorite for general shooting, and particularly for ducks. It is quite simple in its construction and very durable. It loads with

3

a steel shell. There are many other serviceable
guns, recently invented, particularly rifles, where
it is much more difficult to make a choice. For
loons, deer, and larger game, it is well to have
one in the party. Allen's No. 64 is among the
best. These arms are made by Forehand &
Wadsworth, Worcester, Mass., successors to
Ethan Allen & Co. The Winchester possesses
the advantage of rapid firing, and carries seventeen shots, but is much heavier.

Fly-rods, as well as fire-arms, must be purchased in the cities, for there is no certainty of
getting them at the lake. Bradford & Anthony,
186 Washington Street, Boston, and Read &
Sons, 13 Faneuil Hall Square, are well supplied.
As to flies, the red and brown hackle are pre-
ferred. They can be bought in Greenville, to-
gether with apparatus for bait fishing, and spoons
or squids for trolling.

Provisions of all kinds may also be obtained
in Greenville. Mr. Dennen, of the Mt. Kineo
House, frequently finds supplies for parties stop-
ping there. Pork, potatoes, and hard bread are
among the staples for woods fare; but some
carry tin reflectors, and bake their bread by an
open fire. Tea is regarded as a necessity by
every woodsman, at all seasons of the year.

Condensed milk is seldom omitted. Coffee, corn meal, canned fruits and meats, lemons, and other extras are much used. Graham or unbolted wheat meal, and oat meal, can sometimes be procured at the Mt. Kineo House ; but Bangor is the surest place for these and other fancy groceries, including Graham crackers, barley, rice, etc. For meat it is customary to rely on the fish and fowl of the country.

SPORTING SEASON.

August and September are the best months. The game is larger in September, while the weather is more inviting in August, and bathing is one of the attractions. Aside from its chilly nights, October is no wise inferior. Some fishing is done during the latter half of May, after the ice disappears.

The black flies come about the first of June. They begin to disappear early in July, and by the middle are quite scarce. Fishing is fair in this month, but the game is either too young or thin and poor from breeding. A visit in June can be made quite tolerable by keeping on the water or about the clearings near the hotels, where the wind drives the flies into the woods.

It is usual, in camping out at this season, to sleep, eat, and fish aboard the sail boat, and go ashore to cook only. A mixture of oil of tar and pennyroyal is used to besmear the face and hands. Some prefer glycerine and pennyroyal. The clothes should button close, the shirt bosom lap over, and no loop holes be left open, if much time be spent in the woods. Ladies from New York visit the Mt. Kineo House for the June fly-fishing, provided with thin veils.

COST.

The following estimates have been prepared to show that a visit of two weeks can be made from Boston for about fifty dollars. Everything is included except the home outfit and some sporting tackle.

Hotels charge everywhere fifty cents each for meals and room, except the Bangor House and the Mt. Kineo House, where board is two dollars and a half a day. Pullman Palace Sleeping Cars on the Eastern Railroad furnish double berths at two dollars each. The article entitled "Routes from Boston," on page 8, contains much that relates to the subject.

ONE PERSON ONLY.

Two days on the road and twelve at *hotels.*

1. Leaving Boston at 6.20 P.M., pass the night and first day on the road, and stop at Greenville.

2. Eagle Stream and McFarland Place.

3. Wilson Ponds.

4. Steamer to the Outlet, and spend three days.

7. Steamer to the Mt. Kineo House and spend one week, making the ascent of the mountain, fishing in deep water, and exploring the neighborhood.

14. Return home, taking steamer at the hotel wharf, at 5 A.M.

The above programme can be carried out without guide, if desired, but may occasion inconvenience in some instances. The expenses are about as follows, but may be diminished by spending more time at Greenville or the Outlet.

Ticket by rail to Mt. Kineo and return,	15.00
Breakfast and dinner on the road, each way,	2.00
Two and three-quarter days at Greenville,	5.50
Three days at the Outlet,	4.50
One week at the Mt. Kineo House,	15.00
Boat hire, sleeping cars, etc.	8.00
	$50.00

PARTY OF TWO.

Two days on the road, and twelve with *guide and canoe* at three dollars, provisions for all at one dollar per day.

Ticket by rail to Mt. Kineo, and return - - - .	15.00
Guide, etc., at $2.00 per day for each person, - -	24.00
Hotel bills, - - - - - - - - - - - - - - -	6.00
Sleeping cars and other items, - - - - - - - -	5.00
	$50.00

PARTY OF FOUR.

Two days on the road and twelve with *sail boat, two guides, and two canoes*, at eight dollars, and provisions for all at two dollars per day. Moderate economy in the selection of provisions and in regard to the last two items, may reduce this estimate to the proposed standard.

Ticket by rail to Mt. Kineo and return, - - - -	15.00
Sail boat, etc., at $2.50 per day, for each person, -	30.00
Hotel Bills, - - - - - - - - - - - - - - -	6.00
Sleeping cars, and other items. - - - - - - -	5.00
	$56.00

NORTHERN MAINE.

TOURS BEYOND THE LAKE.

ST. JOHN RIVER.

THE most popular trip for those who can afford the time, is that down the St. John River to New Brunswick. It threads the heart of the wilderness, and is made with safety and comfort at the most inviting season of the year. A reliable guide, a stout canoe, a moderate supply of provisions, and a fortnight to spare, are all that is necessary. This, however, would allow no time for recreation on the way, and less than three weeks would hardly satisfy one, while a month can be employed to advantage. For one hundred and fifty miles, from Greenville to the mouth of the Allagash, it is one succession of river and lake, without connected settlements of any kind.

After leaving Moosehead Lake the traveller proceeds to Chesuncook Lake, descending the West Branch of the Penobscot for twenty miles.

The river is still, dark, and deep, or narrow, wild, and rocky by turns. Pine Stream Falls, the only obstacle, is readily descended by a skilful guide ; but it is often necessary to carry some of the luggage along the shore.

At the head of Chesuncook Lake is a settlement of several farms. Mr. Jesse D. Murphy keeps a tavern here that serves as headquarters for the lumbering in this district. We pass the second night with him, or else camp on Umbazooksus Stream, either on its eastern shore at the Cold Spring one mile from its mouth, or at the quarter-of-a-mile carry a mile or two below Umbazooksus Lake. The next day one can cross Mud Pond Carry, and, if all goes well, reach the locks between Chamberlain and Eagle Lakes. Otherwise we can rest at Chamberlain Farm, with its little red house so cosy and comfortable.

Eagle Lake is broken and picturesque. Several small streams, navigable for a short distance, empty into it. It was for many years the haunt of a noted hermit, Donald McDonald, more popularly known as "Dirty Donald."

The Allagash River is the outlet of Eagle and Churchill Lakes. Below the dam is Chase's Carry, by some fearful rapids, one third of a mile in length. At Depot Farm, on Long Lake, resides Mrs. Johnson, with husband and family. She is a half breed, and a famous Amazon of the ancient heroic type. Many stories are told of her masculine energy and endurance. A few miles from the mouth of the Allagash is a sharp pitch, some twenty feet in height. There is some quick water on the river, but nothing dangerous.

On the main St. John are a few bad places, and Great Falls, some seventy miles from the Allagash, is a descent of seventy-five feet, and the main feature of the river. There is one straight pitch of forty feet, and such is the fury of the water that all sawed lumber and square timber must be hauled past. A light suspension bridge for foot passengers crosses the river below, and affords a fine view of the fall. The next sixty miles form a light two days' work on the rapid current. In the spring of the year a steamer traverses this distance, but in summer it goes no farther than Woodstock, where we take passage for Frederic-ton, sixty miles, and the next day by another steamer to St. John, ninety miles. A day may be saved by taking rail. Sometimes the steam-ers do not run above Fredericton.

If parties do not wish to visit the city of St.

John they can take the cars at Woodstock or
Fredericton, for Bangor direct, leaving the former place at 8 A. M., and arriving at 7 P. M., a
distance of one hundred and seventy miles.

There are settlements all the way on the main
St. John, and, instead of keeping on to Great
Falls, parties sometimes turn off some forty miles
or more below the mouth of the Allagash, and
strike northwest across the country to the St.
Lawrence. For the first twenty miles they ascend the Madawaska river, a pretty stream, and
perhaps the finest in the country for a canoe,
being smooth and clear, with gravelly bottom
and a moderate current. Then, crossing Temis-
couata Lake, sixteen miles in length, they take
stage for Rivière du Loup, a settlement on the St.
Lawrence, thirty miles distant. Thence, Quebec
is reached in a day by rail or by steamer.

MT. KATAHDIN.

A fortnight is necessary, but more time is advisable. As by the last route, Chesuncook is
reached on the afternoon of the second day from
Greenville. The third night will be spent at the
three-mile carry below Ripogenus Lake, which
avoids some of the wildest water in the State, a

terror to the river drivers, and known by such pet names as Big and Little Heater, etc. From here two or three days are required to arrive at Sandy Brook, a small stream below Sourdnahunk on the same side of the Penobscot. From the main river to the summit it is some five to seven miles, and parties usually camp half way up. The view, in clear weather, is almost unlimited. Cool springs are found on the side and even near the top. Bears are occasionally met with, and some moose are scattered through the country. The trout fishing in small ponds near Ripogenus Lake and at the mouth of Sourdnahunk Stream, is excellent. Recently large salmon have been taken below the dam at the foot of Chesuncook Lake.

There is a bridle path to Katahdin, from the east. It leaves Golden Ridge, on the Patten stage road, above Mattawamkeag, crosses the East Branch of the Penobscot and the Wassattiquoik, and partly ascends the mountain. Being over land, it lacks the beauty and variety of the other route, although much shorter.

Thoreau's "Maine Woods" and Winthrop's "Life in the Open Air," have described the ascent of Katahdin and the beauties of the Penobscot.

UP THE PENOBSCOT.

There being but few lakes and much shoal water here, this is not a favorite line of travel. It is not without its points of interest, however, and leads one in lonely by-ways. Canada Falls heads the list of its attractions, and the fishing at the mouth of Nulhedus and other streams is excellent.

Parties sometimes go down the St. John this way, crossing over to Baker Lake. The carry into St. John's Pond is preferable to the other, from Abacotnetic Lake, although longer, because there is more water in the Woboostoock than on the other branch.

DOWN THE PENOBSCOT.

The distance from Greenville to Old Town may be traversed in ten days or more. Mt. Katahdin is situated nearly midway, and that route already described is a part of this. Some years since it was the favorite tour of sportsmen, before the St. John River became so well known. It combines more variety than any other, and affords perhaps the best scenery, but has been well nigh abandoned, owing to the extreme fatigue of the many portages. There is said to be

eighteen miles of carries, chiefly by falls and
rapids. The chance for moose is not quite the
best, but aside from the carries above mentioned
it is equal, if not superior, to all other routes.
The many rapids are an obstacle for the guides,
but an attraction for fearless sportsmen.

EAST BRANCH OF THE PENOBSCOT.

We follow the St. John tour to Chamberlain
Lake, then proceed through Telos and Webster
Lakes, down Webster Brook to Grand Lake on
the East Branch. The latter unites with the
West Branch or Main River at Nicatou, a long
way below Katahdin. This avoids some of the
worst places on the Main West Branch, but presents a few difficulties of its own, including the
rough water on Webster Brook and Grand Falls,
about six miles below Grand Lake. Trout Brook
Farm, near Grand Lake, is a convenient place to
rest.

Some eight miles southeast of Grand Lake is
a small pond, on the head of Bowlin Brook, and
tributary to the East Branch, whose waters are
colored milk white from the presence of lime.
A cave in the rock, and partially submerged,
was explored not many years ago by the State
Geological Survey.

CAUCOMGOMOC WATERS,

A group of lakes and ponds, connected by streams for the most part navigable and easy of access from Chesuncook Lake, fourteen miles distant. They are connected with Chamberlain Lake by a carry from Round Pond into Allagash Lake, and may be united with a tour down the St. John or to the East Branch of the Penobscot, occasioning a delay of two days only.

AROOSTOOK RIVER,

Reached by long stage rides, in the eastern part of the State, from Mattawamkeag and Houlton. Its upper branches are generally too shoal for navigation during the dry season.

It may also be approached from the west, by the old Munsungan carry, from Spider Lake, on Allagash Waters, across several small ponds, to the Munsungan Lakes, one of its main sources. This old portage was once quite a thoroughfare, some twenty-five or thirty years ago, before settlements had crept up from the south and after the Lower Aroostook had become the home of thriving communities. It is probable that it was first used by Indians, and later by beaver trappers, and that it fell into disuse as the beaver became rare or less valuable, and other trappers encroached from the south. Many dates before 1850 are found on the trees, and some amused themselves and a subsequent generation, by picturing in red chalk the figure of a man on the dead run, with a canoe on his head, shouting, "Bound for Munsungan," and other devices.

THE MOOSE.

FIRST in size among the animals of Northern Maine and the British Provinces, is the Moose, the largest of the deer species and the most easily domesticated. It is remarkable for its huge proportions, uncouth form, and peaceful habits. Some of the males have been known to measure more than six feet in height at the shoulders, and to exceed one thousand pounds in weight, producing horns, at a certain season of each year, that sometimes weigh fifty pounds. With long legs, a powerful neck, and a large body, it has been said to combine the swiftness of the horse with the strength of the ox. Its flesh is wholesome food, the nose and tongue being regarded as delicacies; its hide, smoke-tanned by the Indians, becomes a pliable leather; and its horns, prized as an article of beauty, might, if plenty, become highly useful.

It is comparatively amiable in its disposition, solitary or domestic in its habits, and a lover of plain fare. In summer it frequents the ponds and streams, feeding on lily pads and water grasses, and taking refuge from its scourge, the moose-fly. Years ago, when numerous, many were killed while feeding in the night time. In winter it selects a favorable spot in some hard wood district, generally on a side hill or in a sheltered valley, and there leisurely strolls about, cropping the twigs of the white wood, moose wood, and other deciduous plants. It thus scours a considerable tract of country, and by its brows- ings may be traced some distance. When the snow is deep it moves with difficulty, and tram- ples down a narrower space, called "the yard."

It is then at the mercy of the hunter on snow shoes. In this way many thousands have been destroyed in the State of Maine alone, during the last twenty years, and only their hides used. Two brothers are known to have killed over eighty in one season, about the year 1862, and left thousands of pounds of good meat to decay in the woods. Such cruel and selfish slaughter has exterminated them in the borders of the forest region ; and it is only by penetrating far into the interior that the scattered remnants are now found. A succession of mild winters en- ables them to multiply, and in some remote dis- tricts become numerous, — but then a fierce cru-

4

sade begins. The Indians cross the boundary
from Canada ; the whites leave the frontier settlements ; and only a few stragglers escape.
The spring of 1869 was noted for its deep snow
and the consequent slaughter of the moose. During the following year some were killed, but not
nearly as many. The springs of 1871 and 1872
were remarkable for the light fall of snow, so that
by the year 1873 they had gained considerably.
In one distant section alone at least seventy were
killed, and all by a few individuals. Two hunters killed nineteen elsewhere ; two others eight
more by scouring a large tract ; and still five
more were killed by two, who were men of too
much humanity and good sense to destroy more
than they could sell to the lumbermen for food.
These are a few facts only that came within the
writer's observation, and form but a part of the
injury done.

Occasionally a hunter is met with who prides
himself in never leaving a quarter of meat to
waste in the woods. And we can the more readily appreciate this spirit after viewing with pain-
ful disgust the selfish indifference of others. If
it were a source of immense profit we might
overlook it in a measure ; but they realize for
each hide only eight or ten dollars at most, and

oftentimes would do better at any honest industry. It is largely a class of men who make their boast that they will not work for any man, but prefer to eke out a scanty subsistence annihilating the treasures of the animal kingdom, in defiance of all law, order, and economy. For the Indians, wasteful and improvident by nature, and now spurred on by competition with the whites, we can have some charity ; but for our hardy trappers there is little excuse.

Sportsmen, too, have in years past destroyed numbers for mere amusement, during the summer season, wantonly sacrificing a noble animal for which they had no possible use. Resident hunters and hard-working men will never give up the profits and pleasures of the chase while strangers can help themselves with impunity. Though from the last we have at present less to fear, yet no partiality should be shown.

The hides are now used for moccasins, and largely exported to the far West. If, as in the case of beaver hats, some substitute should come into use, they might in a measure be spared, at least away from the settlements. But it is hardly probable that they will ever decrease in value, and only the most determined efforts can save them.

There is a law prohibiting their destruction
during a large portion of the year, but, except
when the meat arrives in Bangor, it remains a
dead letter. Certainly it has placed no restraint on
the hunters, and some even assert that it has done
more harm than good, for the time that would
have been better paid in hauling the meat to
market has been devoted to a swift and wholesale
butchery. This may have been true in some
instances, but, for the most part, it is a weak
apology offered by those who regard all law and
authority as so much restraint upon their liber-
ties. The present statute is a *failure*, for two
reasons: *First*, — It is rarely enforced; *Second*, —
It being lawful to kill at one season of the year,
no hides can be seized with certainty. With
sufficient interest in the matter, we can have
ample legislation and men who will execute it.
But without enforcement all laws are a farce,
and throw contempt on the power that created
them.

In Sweden, owing to the scarcity of the moose,
there called elk, it was decided to prohibit their
destruction for ten years.* Here we would be
warranted in doing the same; and, in that case,

*Goodrich's Pictorial Geography, vol. ii. Supplement,
p. 33.

could, within a stated period from the passage of
the law, seize hides as well as meat, wherever
found, at all seasons of the year ; and still later,
perhaps, moccasins also. The coöperation of the
Provinces is needed, so that there shall be no
market for them in North America.

We might have these creatures for our next-
door neighbors, browsing peacefully in the shelter of the woods, and doing harm to no one.
Pigeons live in the crowded streets of our cities,
lazily turning aside for the passing wheel ; yet
it occurs to no one that they are good eating, or
that it would be sport to shoot them.

At the South the vultures have been encour-
aged to enter the cities and do service as scaven-
gers. Droves of hogs run wild in the woods,
and, if they are not molested, it is not because
fresh pork is not a delicacy, or the chase of the
wild boar not an exciting sport.

On the Pacific coast the sea lions bask on the
rocks and sport in the surf in full view of fash-
ionable hotels and numbers of interested specta-
tors. The law protects them, and the public
appreciates its value.

On the Farallon Islands, some precipitous
crags, that rise from the sea, thirty miles west of

San Francisco, thousands of birds annually make
their nests. There are four varieties, and from
one of these alone fifteen to seventeen thousand
dozen of eggs are annually taken to San Francisco, causing no apparent decrease in the number
of the birds or the yield of the eggs ; and all because of a little foresight and system on the part
of the company that has charge of the business.
This takes place chiefly on one small island, the
largest of the group, but not a mile in length
and less than two hundred yards in width, where
a fog-whistle howls its warning, a light-house
gives its blaze by night, and the keepers and
their families reside the year round. Walruses
clamber upon its sides, and rabbits at times become so numerous that famine ensues, while the
birds of one species prey upon the eggs of another. Yet this traffic has been continued for
twenty years, without any diminution, simply
because a sufficient breeding-ground is left undisturbed and the egg-gatherers leave a month
before the birds. When first discovered an eager
strife threatened its destruction, but when, at
last, the parties went armed, the government
interfered, to the benefit of the public at large,
and even of the birds themselves.*

* Harper's Monthly, April, 1874.

On small islands by the coast of Iceland the
eider duck yearly builds its nest, lining it with
the down from its own breast. The eggs furnish food for the natives, and the down is a valuable article of export. Stringent laws and
private ownership have jealously guarded its life
for many generations. Though still a bird of
freedom and migratory in its habits, it has become so tame as to be removed from the nest to
gather the eggs and the lining of eider down.
After this it again plucks the down from its
breast, and again the nest is robbed. The down
of the female is now exhausted, and she calls
upon her mate, who generously responds; then
she lays her eggs once more. Should she be
disturbed for the third time she would forever
quit the spot. We are told by a traveller, that a
woman, who for twenty years had charge of a
district here, increased its yield from fifteen to
one hundred pounds. They made their nests in
holes provided in the huge stone wall, in the
walls of the house even, and one actually settled
by the door scraper. There was scarce a bird
among them all who would not permit her to
remove it from the nest.*

Fabulous numbers of fur seal resort annually

* Hartwig's Polar World, p. 64.

to the largest of four small islands on the coast of Alaska, whose united area is not sixty square miles. This animal is universally deemed shy and difficult of approach, yet here a respectable colony of people is located in plain sight of their breeding ground, much less than a mile distant. For nearly ninety years this has been their only means of support, and has supplied the world, yet there is no decrease of numbers, while the vast area of the Antarctic has been wholly stripped of like resorts by a suicidal lust for plunder. All this is accomplished by the exercise of a little common sense on the part of a few high-minded and sagacious business men. One hundred thousand are selected each year from among the surplus males of two years of age, who are driven from the breeding grounds by the older ones. Their loss is never felt, and thus this marvellous phenomenon is fully preserved in its original condition, while becoming a source of wealth to many, and supplying the world with a rich article of clothing. When first abandoned by the Russians, on the transfer of the territory, private parties began sad havoc, but the government claimed its own, and now derives a handsome revenue from the San Francisco Fur Company, which pays two dollars and a half for each skin, guards the territory, and binds itself to certain limits in the destruction of the animals.*

A similar course of treatment might do the same for our moose, with less outlay than has been expended in the breeding of salmon for our rivers, and with more direct results. They need only be protected where they are. Except man, they have no mortal enemies, not even the wolves, and, multiplying steadily, might soon fill our woods, yielding a convenient supply of food, adding richness to the landscape and wealth to the nation. Their style of life inclines them to narrow limits. They do not migrate, show little inclination to stray off, and can be supported in immense numbers on the vast area that is left vacant for them.

If the territory to be guarded is greater in extent, so will the reward be, and the government should reap any advantage that may accrue, thus diminishing taxes and distributing the profits most equally. The great obstacle is a few men, who would rather see them swept from the face of the earth than give up any privileges, however slight. On the other hand,

* Harper's Monthly. May. 1874.

there are those now engaged who would gladly
see the law enforced, but jealously grasp their
share while it lasts. If once a decided effort
is made, all will follow readily enough. One
determined man of intelligence, stationed at
Chesuncook Farm during the first four months
of the year, and another at Seven Islands,
on the St. John River, might be of great
benefit; but a far more general effort is needed
to afford complete protection.

The *first* step necessary is to arouse a general
interest in the subject; *second*, the enactment of
more stringent laws; *third*, the appointment of
resolute and faithful wardens; *fourth*, the appro-
priation of the requisite sums of money; *fifth*,
and last, the hearty support of the people at
large, without which little will ever be accomplished. Men should be stationed at Greenville,
at Chesuncook and Chamberlain Farms, at Nicatou and Trout Brook Farm on the East Branch,
at Ox Bow on the Aroostook, at Depot Farm on
the Allagash, at Seven Islands on the St. John,
and, in seasons of deep snow, two more should
range the Canadian boundary. With the active
coöperation of the Provinces the work will be
complete, and in a few years less vigilance will
be required. During the summer season, when

the navigable streams are the only means of access, a less number can guard the district.

While the deer is fast disappearing, while the elk has become extinct to the east of the Mississippi, while the bison yearly recedes, and the musk ox has retired beyond the limits of our observation, let us at least preserve this one representative of the northern forest, so near to our very homes, and but a day's journey from the capital of New England.

Hitherto we have considered only the preservation of the moose, as a question of general interest and economy, and one that appeals to our humanity. But neither the love of cruel sport, — an evil in itself, — nor the value of this animal as an article of food and raiment, will suffice to protect it with a people notoriously wasteful of its resources and regardless of the future. Having taken the proper steps to secure its life, we would recommend its domestication, which must be left to individual effort, promoted, perhaps, by State aid.

The moose is identical, or nearly so, with the elk of Northern Europe. In former times, owing to its speed, it was used in Sweden to convey couriers, and is known to have traversed a distance of two hundred and thirty-four miles in one day, attached to a sleigh. Later, when Europe regarded its use with interest, having been taken to aid in the escape of criminals, its domestication was prohibited, so dangerously successful did their narrow minds regard the first experiments.*

The reindeer, drawing its master in his snug sled, with such rapidity over the snow fields of Lapland, is a familar picture to the mind of every child. The woodland caribou of North America is the same or a similar variety, and yet both are said to be less easy of domestication than the moose, which is superior in strength, like frugal in habits, and equally adapted to the severity of the winter's cold. Unlike the horse, it needs no stable, no bed, and provides its own store of food at all seasons of the year. Taken young, it becomes readily attached ; and while still enjoying its freedom, continues to acknowledge allegiance to its new master, thus meeting him more than half way in the novel experiment.

It has been urged that the older ones show some signs of ugliness, and even become quite unmanageable. Yet, perhaps, no stronger argu-

*Goodrich's Pictorial Geography, vol. ii. Supplement, p. 33.

ment of unfitness for man's use could be found
than the utter lack of spirit in beings that have
ever ranged the forest, wild and independent.

The dog, in its savage state, by its irritable
disposition, so dangerous to all other forms of
life, has become the most affectionate and faithful of domesticated animals, though closely allied
to the wolf and the fox, among the fiercest of
carnivori. Man's teaching has even supplanted
instinct, and the pointer is born with an absurd
tendency to point at game instead of seizing it,
thus serving its master's interest rather than its
own. The records of ancient Egypt prove to us
that cats went hunting with their masters, and
even entered the water in pursuit of game.*
But what could be expected of the horse, even,
when first taken from its native wilds? Or of the
stupid ox, if it had always enjoyed its freedom?
For countless generations man has been mould-
ing their dispositions to suit his needs ; and yet
it is well known with what difficulty and danger
the use of the perfect male of both species is
attended.

For centuries the reindeer has been the sole
support of many northern tribes, furnishing
them with food, clothing, shelter, and a means

*Atlantic Monthly, May, 1874.

of conveyance. Yet by kindness alone it is kept in submission. Its master dares not strike it harshly, neither give it too heavy a load, lest it turn and attack him with fore-feet and horns, when he is obliged to hide under his upturned sled until its rage cools. Such a seeming sense of justice, united with an affectionate disposition, betokens more than ordinary intelligence, and leads us to expect much of the deer family.

When Europeans first visited these shores they were welcomed by the simple natives, who recognized at once the superiority of intellect. Like children, they confided in their honor, treated them with veneration, and acceded to all their proposals. At last, exasperated by treachery and wanton abuse, they learned to fear and then hate that civilization which they had so much admired. Crime, misery, and death, were the result.

The dictates of the heart, and the stern principles of justice, have alike failed to teach us the lessons of humanity. To cold policy alone is left the task. As a people, we are enterprising and industrious, yet seem to possess but little patience, unless prompted by the love of money, or that kindred quality, the love of its

* Hartwig's Polar World, p. 20.

display. On the one hand, careworn and weary, there are those who consider only their daily bread. On the other, there are the wealthy, who lavish on themselves and on their estates a regal magnificence, yet are no happier than those in humble homes. While art receives every encouragement, and we worship at the shrine of beauty in all its forms, let us not forget that which, bringing to our doors curious and wonderful beings, shall multiply our resources, testify to our humanity, beautify the earth, and do honor to our civilization.

OTHER ANIMALS.

AME is found throughout the extent of country covered by the map. Moose, as may already be inferred, exist in small numbers through the northern half. Caribou, or reindeer, wander from one end to the other. Deer abound in spots in the southern and eastern portions. Bears are scattered in all parts, particularly in rocky or mountainous districts. Wolves, alone or in groups, and single foxes, prowl about. While the beaver, otter, mink, sable, and other fur-bearing animals, furnish a partial means of support to numbers of trappers. Ducks, partridges, and fish, are the chief reliance for food. But the trout, which everywhere abound, are the first attraction.

MAP.

THE Map has been prepared from many reliable sources, and covers a large area of uninhabited territory.

The one great advantage for travellers, possessed by this tract of wilderness, is its navigable waters. . Short carries, or portages, unite the different river systems, and few points are so remote that they cannot be approached by water with canoe and an ample outfit.

Without its timber this country would remain unexplored, and the few farms that lie scattered at long intervals serve either as taverns on the main routes of winter travel, or to raise supplies in the centre of some lumbering district, to save the enormous expense of hauling them from the settlements.

The only roads passable for teams in summer are those about the foot of the lake, the Canada road to the west of it, and a strip seven miles in length from Lily Bay to Roach River. The rest are called "tote roads," to distinguish them from the short logging roads, which, of course,

could not be given on any map. They are used
in winter only to haul supplies on the snow to
the lumbermen's camps. Only a part of these
are open each season, and all are liable to change
in some portion to suit the location of the camps.
It is surprising what an amount of work has been
performed in the woods. Logging roads are
everywhere met with, varying in age from those
of the previous winter to the faint traces, in
decayed logs and bush-grown paths, of a former
generation.

The carries are shown on the map as far as
practicable, and the mountains when quite large
and sufficiently well known. All the streams
of any importance and most of the ponds are
given.

Special Notices.

ROUTES.

HOTELS.

STORES.

EASTERN & MAINE CENTRAL R. R. LINE.

THE only line making direct connections without change of cars between Boston and Bangor. Pullman Sleeping Cars on Night Trains. Passengers leaving Boston at 8.15 A.M., arrive at Dexter the same evening, take stage the next morning for Greenville, at foot of the Lake, where a steamer is in waiting to convey passengers to the Mt. Kineo House. in the centre of the Lake, arriving at 6 P.M. Or, leaving at 6.20 P.M. by the Night Train, they proceed via. E. & M. C. R.R. line to Bangor, thence via. Stage and Steamer as above, and arrive at the same hour. [Distances on page 8.]

Fare for the round trip, $15.00. Tickets can be obtained in Boston at 134 Washington Street, at the Depot, and at the Mt. Kineo House at the Lake.

This is the only line making direct and sure connections and issuing through tickets between Boston and all points in the State of Maine and the maritime Provinces. Baggage checked through. Only one change of cars between Boston and St. John, and two between Boston and Halifax.

CHAS. F. HATCH,   J. W. CLAPP,   GEO. F. FIELD,
Gen. Manager.   *Gen. Tick. Agt. M. C. R. R.*   *Gen. Pass. Agt.*

Sanford's Independent Line,

BETWEEN Boston and Bangor, connecting with the EUROPEAN & NORTH AMERICAN RAILWAY, for MOOSEHEAD LAKE and intermediate stations. Also, for Houlton, St. John, Halifax, etc. *Fares lower than by any other route. Excursion Tickets from Boston to Mt. Kineo and return, $13.00 : Single Tickets, $7.00,* From Boston to Bangor, $3.00 ; from Boston to Greenville, Moosehead Lake, $6.00. Two steamers on the route, and four trips a week each way, touching at all the principal landings on the Penobscot River and Bay. The steamers Cambridge, Capt. J. P. Johnson, and Katahdin, Capt. W. R. Roix,

Leave Boston, Rowe's Wharf, at 5 P.M.

Mondays, Tuesdays, Thursdays and Fridays.

Leave Bangor at 11 A.M.

Mondays, Wednesdays, Thursdays and Saturdays.

AGENTS.

W. B. HAZELTINE,   LOOMIS TAYLOR,
Boston.   *Bangor.*

69

FRYE'S STAGE LINE

FOR

MOOSEHEAD LAKE.

—

FINE SCENERY AND A RAPID TRANSIT.

LEAVES DEXTER at 8 A.M.; meets the Bangor train, at GUILFORD, at 11 A. M.; and reaches GREENVILLE at 4 P. M., to connect with the

STEAM-YACHT TWILIGHT,

FOR THE

MT. KINEO HOUSE.

THE Twilight arrives at 6 P. M.. and leaves the hotel wharf at 5 A. M., each day, to connect, by stage, with the trains at Guilford and Dexter.

———

THROUGH TICKETS purchased in Boston at

BOSTON AND MAINE DEPOT, and

ROWE'S WHARF, SANFORD'S STEAMERS.

THE LAKE.

STEAMER GOV. COBURN.

CAPT. THOMAS ROBINSON.

THE largest on the Lake, and launched in 1872. Leaves Greenville every morning, at 8 o'clock, for the Mt. Kineo House, touching at any desired point on the route. Visits the head of the Lake on Tuesdays and Fridays, and daily during the blueberry season. Agent, D. T. SANDERS, Greenville.

STEAM-YACHT DAY-DREAM.

MT. KINEO HOUSE.

THIS little Steamer is kept as a pleasure boat for the use of the guests at the Mt. Kineo House. It is covered with a light roof, open at the sides, and contains a snug cabin, with dining table; also apparatus for cooking by steam. May be hired, with captain, engineer, and fuel, for ten dollars per day.

Address O. A. DENNEN, Superintendent of the Mt. Kineo House.

71

YACHT CHALLENGE

CAPT. SAMUEL COLE.

LARGEST on the Lake, a sloop of twenty-six feet keel. With one guide, six dollars per day; five for long trips. With two guides, eight dollars per day. Canoes, tents, blankets, and cooking tools included. Also, other Sail Boats, Row Boats, and Canoes to let. Mounted Deer Horns for sale.

Capt. Cole is a hunter of experience, and acts as guide to all parts of Northern Maine and the Provinces. Other competent guides supplied on short notice, and any general information.

Address, SAMUEL COLE, Greenville, Maine.

YACHT SAILOR-BOY.

CAPT. FRANK VAUGHN.

A CENTRE-BOARD sloop of twenty-one feet keel, new, and a fast sailer. Takes out parties with guide and canoe, for five dollars per day. Tents, blankets, and cooking tools included.

Address, FRANK VAUGHN, Greenville, Me.

Hotels.

NEWPORT.

SHAW HOUSE.

CHARLES SAWYER.

SPACIOUS and cheerful, with pleasant surroundings. Equal to any hotel between Bangor and Mt. Kineo. A short distance across the field, to the rear, lies Newport Pond, very large, with good perch and pickerel fishing.

On the return from Moosehead Lake, via Dexter, by the night train, a *delay of two hours and forty minutes*, from 6.15 to 8.55 P. M., allows ample time to take supper at the hotel and stroll about the place. Those who travel by daylight only can *avoid* the hurry of *an early start* from Dexter, at 7.45 A. M., by passing the night here and leaving at 9.15 A. M.

Conveyance free, to and from the depot.

73

DEXTER.

MERCHANTS EXCHANGE.

L. D. HAYES.

NEW and comfortable, near the centre of business in the heart of the town. Hack to and from the trains. Livery Stable connected. Stages leave daily for Moosehead Lake, thirty-five miles distant; also for Dover and other points. Through passengers receive good fare and prompt attention.

Dexter is a busy town of about three thousand inhabitants, the terminus of a branch railway, and at the outlet of a large pond among the hills, that affords water power for several factories. It is 233 miles from Boston, and 14 from Newport by rail. The *Boston Express* arrives each day, at 10.20, A.M., and 7.35, P.M. Leaves at 7.45, A.M., and 5.30, P. M.

BANGOR.

PENOBSCOT EXCHANGE.

ABRAM WOODARD.

L ARGE and convenient, on Exchange Street, near the business centre, a few steps from the European Depot. A first-class house, the resort of travellers and business men. Meals served at 7, 1 and 6. Board, two dollars per day.

DEPARTURE OF TRAINS.

MAINE CENTRAL DEPOT.

For Boston, at 8.00, A. M,. and 7.45, P. M.

EUROPEAN & NORTH AMERICAN DEPOT.

(Two minutes' walk from the Hotel.)

For Oldtown and Guilford, at 7, A. M., and 5.10, P. M.

Mattawamkeag, at 8.00, A. M., and 8.00, P. M.

St. John, Houlton, and Calais, at 8.00, A. M.

TURNER HOUSE.

Z. L. TURNER.

AT the terminus of the Piscataquis Branch Railway. The routes to Moosehead Lake in winter unite here. A good dinner of several courses is then served each day, to numbers of through passengers. Good pickerel fishing in two ponds, one mile and a half distant. Pleasant drives in the river valley. Board, two dollars per day.

MONSON.

CHAPIN HOUSE.

A. W. CHAPIN.

ON the verge of the great northern forest, and midway of the stage route to Moosehead Lake. A mountainous forest country stretches away to the right and left. Hebron Pond, not two hundred feet from the house, winds among the hills to the west. Other large trout ponds lie among the hills to the east not far distant.

Monson is a cluster of tidy dwellings, new and snow-white, built after the fire, but a few years since. Several slate quarries, recently opened on the outskirts, are making rapid progress.

76

EVELETH HOUSE.

WM. H. MITCHELL.

OPPOSITE the Post Office, on an elevation commanding the lake. In the cool shade of the piazza, with breezes from the water, a view of the islands and Squaw Mountain may be enjoyed to advantage. The house is conducted in a first-class manner, with clean and comfortable rooms and a well-furnished table. Horses and carriages, also boats, can be had to enjoy the pleasant drives and the beauties of the lake.

LAKE HOUSE.

SAWYER & SAVAGE.

RECENTLY enlarged, with accommodations for one hundred guests; also private parlor, reading room, and hair dressing saloon, A double piazza extends the length of the front and the lake sides of the house. The steamboat wharf and store are close by. Several small boats are at the disposal of the guests. A livery stable is connected. Conveyance to and from Wilson Pond at all hours.

—

MORRIS FARM.

WEST BRANCH.

JOSEPH MORRIS.

TWO miles from Moosehead Lake, by the Northeast Carry. Lies in the midst of fertile meadows, by the side of the Penobscot. Seeboomook Falls is a romantic spot, four miles to the west, and the same distance to the east is Lobster Pond, noted for the variety of its scenery and the profusion of its pond lilies. Mr. Morris is always present, with wagon, on the arrival of the steamer, to haul canoes and luggage across the carry.

CHESUNCOOK FARM.

CHESUNCOOK LAKE.

JESSE D. MURPHY.

AT the head of Chesuncook Lake, in full view of Mt. Katahdin, reached by river from Moosehead Lake, twenty miles distant. A central location, in the neighborhood of many delightful streams. From here parties may visit Mt. Katahdin or pursue their way down the St. John River in the heart of the moose country.

Stores.

BRADFORD & ANTHONY,

186 WASHINGTON STREET,

FISHING TACKLE AND FANCY HARDWARE.

FISHING.

RODS.	HOOKS,	NETS,
REELS.	FLIES,	BASKETS,
LINES,	BAITS,	ETC. ETC.

SUITED TO ALL WATERS.

CUTLERY.

SHEFFIELD CUTLERY,

AMERICAN TABLE CUTLERY.

SCISSORS, KNIVES, AND RAZORS.

FANCY GOODS.

DRESSING CASES,	BAGS,
DRAWING INSTRUMENTS,	RULES,
DOG COLLARS,	BELLS.

SKATES AND SKATE STRAPS.

GUIDES AND MAPS OF MOOSEHEAD LAKE.

BOSTON.

ARTHUR J. COLBURN,

486 WASHINGTON ST.

NATURALIST & TAXIDERMIST,

BIRD EMPORIUM.

ANIMALS, BIRDS, FISHES, DEER'S HEADS, &C. Prepared, Stuffed, and Mounted to order, in the most skilful manner. ARTIFICIAL EYES for Birds and Animals, wholesale and retail.

Birds, Bird Skins, Insect Pins, Choice Singing Canaries, Cages, Goldfish, Globes, Aquaria Tanks, Leaves, Cork, Glass Shades, &c. Mounted HORNS of all kinds.

Send stamp for Catalogue.

A. WILLIAMS & CO.

135 WASHINGTON ST.

MAPS, ATLASES, AND GLOBES.

MOUNTED MAPS for Offices and Libraries, of every portion of the world, and especially of the different States of our own country.

POCKET MAPS FOR TRAVELLERS AND TOURISTS.

In great variety, embracing general maps of the whole United States, and special maps of single States and Territories.

83

GREENVILLE.

POST OFFICE

AT THE STORE OF

JOHN H. EVELETH & CO.

DEALERS IN

Groceries, Household Goods, & Farming Tools,

SPECIAL attention given to supplying *Sportsmen* with Provisions, Canned Fruits, &c. An assortment of Fishing Tackle, Fly Hooks, and Pocket Compasses.

D. T. SANDERS & CO.

DEALERS IN

Groceries, Fishing Tackle, Cutlery, & Canoes.

SPORTSMEN supplied with every convenience except Guns and Fly Rods. A constant supply of Shot, Powder, and Caps; Fly Hooks; Squids and Spoons for Trolling; Tackle of all sizes for Bait Fishing. Also the strongest Ready-made Clothing, Rubber Coats, and Overalls.

Canoes for sale, or *to let* at twenty-five cents per day.

85

NEW YORK.

CHAS. REICHE & BRO.,

55 CHATHAM.

BIRDS & ANIMALS,

Fowls and Mocking Bird Food.

HIGHEST price paid for live specimens of the *Beaver, Otter, Bear, Wild Cat, Moose, Elk, Antelope,* and all kinds of wild American animals and birds.

Alfeld, Germany,	*New York,*	*Boston,*
CHAS. REICHE.	HENRY REICHE,	C. F. HOLDEN

87

FOREST AND STREAM.

A WEEKLY JOURNAL, DEVOTED TO LEGITIMATE SPORTS.

Published in New York: 17 Chatham Street (City Hall Square).

Philadelphia: 125 South Third Street.

[See preceding page.]

W92.

www.ingramcontent.com/pod-product-compliance
Lightning Source LLC
Chambersburg PA
CBHW020314090426
42735CB00009B/1339